IMAGES
of America

LAYTON

This is a mid-1940s aerial view of Layton that reveals the enormous size of Verdeland Park (bottom housing cluster). In 1943, approximately 1,440 residents lived in 400 housing units there on 85 acres. With World War II raging, hundreds of civilian workers came to Layton to work in the defense industry at Hill Field and the Navy Supply Depot in Clearfield and lived in this federal housing. When Verdeland Park was being built, Layton's total population was only 960. Eventually, the 85 acres became Layton Commons Park, Layton High School, and Layton Municipal Center. (Courtesy of Heritage Museum of Layton.)

ON THE COVER: The Layton Farmer's Union Building, at 12 South Main Street, is shown in a wintertime picture of the 1910s. The people in front of the bank may be E.P. Ellison, Farmer's Union superintendent, and some family members. The frame store opened in 1882 as the Kaysville Farmer's Union. There was a dance hall upstairs, and that feature led to many marriages in town. Later, apartments opened upstairs, along with dentist R.C. Robinson's office, which operated from 1922 to 1968. There was also a connecting wooden annex building (not shown) on the left (south) side of the main building for many years. At the corner of Main and Gentile Streets, Farmer's Union operated until 1957. First National Bank of Layton moved into the building in 1981, and now it houses First Community Bank Utah. Given Layton's agricultural roots, this former business that catered to farmers, as well as Layton City's modern prowess as a regional retail hub, makes this approximate-century-old store picture on the book's cover very appropriate. (Courtesy of Heritage Museum of Layton.)

IMAGES
of America

LAYTON

Lynn Arave

ARCADIA
PUBLISHING

Published by Arcadia Publishing
Charleston, South Carolina

Printed in the United States of America

Library of Congress Control Number: 2019955559

For all general information, please contact Arcadia Publishing:
Telephone 843-853-2070
Fax 843-853-0044
E-mail sales@arcadiapublishing.com
For customer service and orders:
Toll-Free 1-888-313-2665

Visit us on the Internet at www.arcadiapublishing.com

To the people of Layton

CONTENTS

ACKNOWLEDGMENTS

The author especially thanks Bill Sanders, museum curator at the Heritage Museum of Layton, for collecting and scanning the majority of the photographs in this book and for his extensive historical knowledge. The museum already had most of the pictures contained herein in its large collection.

Unless otherwise noted, all images in this book appear courtesy of the Heritage Museum of Layton.

Also, many thanks and appreciation are due to Harris Adams, a longtime Layton historian, for his remarkable knowledge and expertise. At age 90, Harris still has a keen memory, and his reflections of Layton's history—and some photographs from his collection—proved invaluable to this book.

The 1985 book *Layton, Utah Historical Viewpoints*, by the Kaysville-Layton Historical Society, was relied upon heavily for reference in this work and is recommended for anyone wanting to further study Layton's history. The Heritage Museum of Layton is another great local history resource.

The Utah Division of State History also provided some photographs for this book from its digital collection.

Several family members of the author, including sons Roger Arave and Taylor Arave, plus daughter-in-law Whitney Arave, contributed photographs to this book and other assistance. The author's wife, LeAnn Flygare Arave, also contributed valuable advice on the book.

Note that the author also maintains several historical blogs on Google, including *Mystery of Utah History* and *Layton, Utah History*. Their content supplemented some material in this book.

In addition, as a matter of disclosure, the author was employed on a limited part-time basis as a news specialist for Layton City Corporation when he wrote this book.

INTRODUCTION

Layton is a Western community with a strong pioneer heritage and marked its 100th birthday as an official city in 2020. It is named after Christopher Layton, an early pioneer and church leader in Layton.

Layton, Utah, is by far the largest of the four total Laytons in the United States and the only one in the west. (The other three Laytons are in Florida, New Jersey, and North Dakota.)

Layton is located in the northern section of the Salt Lake Valley, bordered by the Wasatch Mountains to the east and the Great Salt Lake to the west. Salt Lake City is 23 miles south, and Ogden is some 11 miles north.

The Layton area and Salt Lake Valley is an old lake bed for ancient Lake Bonneville, which covered the land with fresh water up to 1,000 feet deep. The Great Salt Lake is a remnant of Lake Bonneville.

There are six major creeks within Layton City's borders, some with smaller tributaries. It was these sources that gave early pioneers their water.

The elevation difference in the Layton area goes from Thurston Peak, east of the city (and highest in Davis County), 9,706 feet above sea level, down to approximately 4,280 feet on its extreme western side.

Layton is also known for its seasonal sentinel on the mountainside each spring—the "Snow Horse." Deep gullies naturally create a horse-like shape each late May into early June on average. This figure was a pioneer landmark each spring, and if any part of it remained into July, it meant continuous water all summer from the streams that flow into Layton from the Wasatch Mountains.

The climate in Layton is one of four seasons and receives an average of about 22 inches of moisture annually. Historically, Layton's hottest month is July, and the coldest is January. Its wettest month is April, and July is the driest. The hottest temperature ever recorded in Layton City was 105 degrees. This has happened twice: on July 14, 2002, and July 18, 1998. Layton has reached 104 degrees on two other occasions: on July 19, 1998, and July 4, 2001.

Although no exact temperature records were kept in Layton in the early 1930s, its coldest day ever was likely either February 9 or February 10 in 1933, at probably around minus 30 degrees.

December 25–31, 2003, was likely Layton's snowiest-ever-recorded period, when the east bench of Layton received 51 inches of snow.

Like most of Davis County, gusting canyon winds in excess of 100 miles per hour during the spring and fall periodically plague Layton too. It is rare, but several tornadoes have also touched the ground in Layton over its recorded history.

Layton is one of Utah's 10 largest cities and is the biggest in Davis County, having overtaken Bountiful in population in 1985. Layton's population was approaching 80,000 in 2019. The city covers 22.49 square miles and has 315.5 miles of city streets.

The community began as an agricultural area, bolstered by the completion of the Davis and Weber County Canal in 1885 and East Canyon Reservoir in 1899. Two different railroad lines through town also made for handy produce and livestock shipping, as well as transportation.

Layton developed a robust downtown business area early on and boasted a few major industries in the early 20th century: the Layton Sugar Factory and the Layton Roller Mills (flour).

Layton is an outgrowth of neighboring Kaysville. It became a separate community in 1902 and incorporated as a city on May 24, 1920.

World War II totally changed Layton (and surrounding communities) forever and began the trend to shift the town away from a farming and ranching mecca, tripling its population. Hill Field, a military airbase located partially in Layton, ramped up and soon became the state of Utah's largest employer.

Modern Layton is also the product of three different cities. The town of Laytona was annexed into Layton in 1957, and East Layton City merged with Layton in 1984.

The Fort Lane Shopping Center arrived in 1963, with Safeway, Kings, and Layton Drug, to give residents their first modern shopping area.

Davis Hospital began in 1976, and Kmart was Layton's first big box store, opening in 1978. The Layton Hills Mall started a business boon in town beginning in 1980.

Smith's Food Production and Distribution Center arrived in 1985, and Layton City opened its Surf 'n Swim facility a year later.

By the 1990s, Layton was well known for its "Restaurant Row," a collection of many popular eateries. By 1991, it had its first Walmart, followed by a Sam's Club in 1994, and a Neighborhood Walmart version located in town during 2004.

In the decades that followed, Layton gained its own satellite campus of Weber State University, the Davis County Conference Center, and a second major hospital, Intermountain Layton Hospital.

Hill Air Force Base (AFB) remains a hallmark of Layton. The "Sound of Freedom"—jets flying over portions of the city—is often heard. Many residents work on base, and Layton is also a bedroom community for many others who are employed in Salt Lake County or elsewhere along the Wasatch Front.

Three of Layton City's largest annual celebrations are the Fourth of July (Liberty Days), Taste of the Town on July 24 (Pioneer Day), and holiday lights in Commons Park (starting the Monday night before Thanksgiving Day and continuing through January 1).

In addition, Layton maintains the Surf 'n Swim, a wave pool enclosed in a bubble (and outdoors in the summer); sponsors a wide variety of family events and recreational programs annually; boasts 13 city parks; and has a heritage museum, the Vietnam Memorial Wall replica, and the Ed Kenley Amphitheater.

Adams Canyon is a popular hiking paradise located east of Layton. The US Forest Service's Fernwood Picnic area is another outdoor asset. The city also maintains numerous hiking and biking trails.

Layton City is governed by a council/manager form of government. The Layton City Council is composed of five members and a mayor. All members are elected by the residents of the city during a municipal election held every two years. Each seat consists of a four-year term. Council member terms are staggered. Two members and a mayor are elected at one time, and two years later, the other three members are elected. The mayor and council are responsible for setting city policy, and the city manager is responsible for the day-to-day operations.

The mission statement of Layton City is to provide services and opportunities, in partnership with the community, that enhance the quality of life.

As this book goes to press, Layton will soon be adding another asset, a local temple for the Church of Jesus Christ of Latter-day Saints (LDS). This will be the second such edifice in Davis County and the 19th in Utah. It will be at the corner of Oak Hills Drive and Rosewood Lane. It will sit on 11.8 acres and will be a three-story, 87,000-square-foot building.

Note: this book is only a snapshot of Layton's rich history, based on available space. Sadly, as such, not every business, church, school, historical event, or aspect of Layton City could be included.

One

EARLY YEARS

Occasional findings of ancient tools and relics in Layton prove that Native Americans lived in the area hundreds of years before white settlers arrived. Also, there were small bands of Native Americans living in the area when settlers arrived.

Like most northern Utah communities, Layton was settled by early pioneers from the Church of Jesus Christ of Latter-day Saints and was the 37th such area to be homesteaded.

Three pioneers—Edward Phillips, William Kay, and John H. Green—and their families first visited the area in 1849 and returned to settle in settled in the spring of 1850. (Some histories claim it was 1849.) Others followed that year. (Christopher Layton, the city's namesake, moved to the area in 1852.)

Layton was an outgrowth of Kaysville, and thus, its streets were not as meticulously planned or square-shaped as they were in many Latter-day Saint communities. The Layton name also did not take hold for almost four decades. It was called Kays Crossing at first. (Layton had also briefly been called Little Fort since Kaysville had a larger one.)

In fact, the very first newspaper reference to Layton being its own community, separate from mother Kaysville City, was published on May 7, 1886, in the *Ogden Herald* newspaper. "The town of Layton is building up rapidly," the *Herald* stated. "There is good demand for everything a farmer raises."

Besides Layton residents wanting their own community, they were very discontented over their taxes from Kaysville City, with little or no benefits to them. Dog licensing was another issue. These controversies exploded in 1899 when Ephraim P. "E.P." Ellison, a prominent businessman, led extensive legal battles to separate from Kaysville. This legal battle not only went to the Utah Supreme Court but the US Supreme Court as well. In 1902, Layton won and became an unincorporated area of Davis County—and also boasted its own growing business district at that time.

Christopher Layton was the first Latter-day Saint bishop in what is now Layton. In 1892, it was officially accepted that Layton be the community's name to honor the early leader.

Layton was incorporated as a third-class town on May 24, 1920, with approximately 500 residents.

Jim Bridger June 1934

1934

Del Adams of Layton rode in the Pioneer Day Parade in Salt Lake City on July 24, 1934. Adams portrayed mountain man Jim Bridger in many events over the decades, continuing into the 1960s. Adams was also a well-known hunter. He died in 1971 at age 81. Some histories claim Bridger visited Layton territory in 1825 as perhaps one of the first white men to ever set foot there.

Christopher Layton is Layton City's namesake. The multitalented pioneer was also a colonizer, settler, statesman, farmer, industrialist, and church leader. Born in 1821, Layton was a member of the Mormon Battalion, an early settler, and Latter-day Saint bishop. He died in 1898 at the age of 77.

This is a historical marker located in Layton, this one on a large rock in front of the Heritage Museum of Layton. Like most early Utah communities, this fort was built for protection against Native Americans. Since Kaysville boasted a larger fort, Layton's was dubbed "Little Fort." It was constructed where today's Fort Lane is and is the source of that name.

This is a rare photograph featuring five of Layton's early settlers, probably taken in 1861. From left to right are (first row) Elias Adams Jr., John Q. Adams, and Joseph S. Adams; (second row) Rufus Adams and George W. Adams. Elias was only 18 in the picture and built a cabin on Gentile Street. John and Rufus both moved to Genoa, Nevada. George was one of the leading landowners in town, and Samuel had a profitable 80-acre farm in the Layton area. (Courtesy of Harris Adams.)

This is the Joseph "Cap" Hill cabin at its original location next to Kays Creek, near the Kaysville border. It was associated with the westward movement of California gold seekers during the Utah settlement era. It was built between 1851 and 1856 and illustrates how early settlers lived. The Hill cabin is also the only settlement-era cabin in Davis County that sat in its original location for over 161 years.

This is a newer picture of the Joseph "Cap" Hill cabin, built by Joseph and Ann Marston Hill, now residing next to the Heritage Museum of Layton, inside Commons Park. The building was restored in 1990 and moved to the museum in 2017. It is a rare example of log cabin construction from the earliest white settlements of the Salt Lake Valley. (Author photograph.)

Yampatch Wongan Timbimboo was a Shoshoni Native American who lived in Northern Utah during Layton's early history. Besides the Shoshoni, some Utah Utes also lived in the same regions of Salt Lake, Weber, and Ogden Valleys and together totaled about 800 persons in the year 1865. Some were survivors of the Bear River Massacre of 1863. Indian tales in Layton are few, but a band of Native Americans lived near Dawson Hollow and Cherry Lane in the 1850s.

Yampatch Wongan Timbimboo
1863 to 1929.

This is a portion of a 19th-century flour mill from Kaysville, back when Layton was part of Kaysville. This relic now sits outside the northwest corner of the Heritage Museum of Layton. (Author photograph.)

Wooden wagon wheels like this were a fixture during the early decades of life in the Layton area and the rest of the West. Layton's first two businesses, John Green's Stage Coach Station and Stables, as well as Christopher Layton's Prairie House Stagecoach Inn, both opened in 1857 and relied heavily on the wagon wheel. The wheel in this picture is preserved as part of the Heritage Museum of Layton. (Author photograph.)

The Layton Roller Mills, at 18 South Main Street, was opened in 1890 by Ephraim P. Ellison, Henry Gibson, and others. In 1895, up to three railroad cars full of flour were shipped from the mill every day. In its 1903 heyday, it could produce and fill 440 sacks of flour a day, more than any other mill in Utah. The mill burned down in 1951, and a service station replaced it on the property. The whiteness in the picture is caused by the thick flour dust in the air.

This is the Farmer's Union general mercantile store at 12 South Main Street. The north section was constructed in 1892 and was refurbished and expanded over the decades. The Farmer's Union closed in 1957. First Community Bank Utah now uses the building. Note the railroad tracks in front of the building, as they were a spur line that existed until 1952.

Elias Adams Jr. (center) stands with family members at his home in eastern Layton in 1897. Two of his hired farmhands are on the far left. Born in Payson, Adams County, Illinois, Adams was six when he crossed the plains to Utah in an 1850 Wagon train. His father, Elias Sr., is the namesake for Adams Canyon. (Courtesy of Harris Adams.)

Elias Adams, Jr. Family and Home Layton, Utah 1914

Catherine Maria   Rufus William   George Winfield   Jabez Samuel   Joshua Isaac   Lettie May, widow
Dennis Elias   Ella Rose   Esther Ann   Elizabeth Belinda   Clyde B.   Ruth Ellen   Clair John

The Elias Adams Jr. family poses in their Layton yard, likely following the funeral of their father in 1912. Adams died on August 29 of that year at age 69. He was buried in the Kaysville Cemetery and had 10 children. Layton shared the Kaysville Cemetery for many decades. (Courtesy of Harris Adams.)

LAYTON WILL GO IT ALONE

Judge Rolapp Enters a Decree at Farmington Separating the Davis County Village From the City of Kaysville--End of a Long Contention.

Judge Rolapp entered a decree in the District Court at Farmington this morning which materially reduces the extent, taxable property and population of Kaysville.

Until this morning Layton has been a suburb of Kaysville within the taxable limits but enjoying none of the benefits of fire and police systems.

For the past fifteen years the citizens of Layton have objected to this condition of things. They objected to paying taxes into the city treasury of Kaysville and deriving no benefit therefrom. Their indignation increased until they decided they would not pay taxes and in this position they were sustained by a decision of the Supreme court which held that the boundaries of a city could not extend farther than the protection of their fire and police systems and that the citizens of Layton one and one-fourth miles from Kaysville switch were not legally bound to pay taxes into the city treasury of Kaysville. And so the Laytonites continued to hold on to their hard-earned sheckels.

But the supreme court, some time ago, in the Grantsville case reversed this decision and then the Laytonites found they were owing about $1000 for back city taxes and their property had been sold as delinquent.

By this time the citizens of Kaysville proper had become weary of the litigation and they petitioned for a restriction of the city's boundaries. The Layton people also filed a similar petition. A commission was appointed and an agreement entered into which is practically a victory for the people of Kaysville as the separation of Layton took place according to a proposition advanced by them, and Judge Rolapp has entered a decree accordingly.

The agreement is that the people of Layton pay all delinquent city taxes to Kaysville, that Kaysville retains all city property and assumes all liabilities, that two-sevenths of the property in the contested Layton district remain in the city and five-sevenths in Layton and one-third the population of that district remains in the city and two-thirds in Layton. Thus Layton proper is only five-sevenths as large as to taxable property and two-thirds as large as to population.

Brown & Henderson were attorneys for the Layton people and C. C. Richards for the Kaysville people.

This is one of the most important media reports in all of Layton's history. This article from the *Ogden Daily Standard* newspaper of March 1, 1902, explains the legal decision that allowed Layton to separate from Kaysville City. Layton residents still had to pay all past due taxes to Kaysville, but this ended more than 20 years of dispute on the issue.

Layton's First National Bank was heavily damaged by a canyon high wind event in its first few months of operation in 1905. The bank was speedily rebuilt as a stronger structure. These howling east winds periodically hit Layton and the Wasatch Front, especially in the spring and fall. Wind speeds have reached more than 100 miles per hour during some canyon events and have even toppled railroad cars and semitrucks.

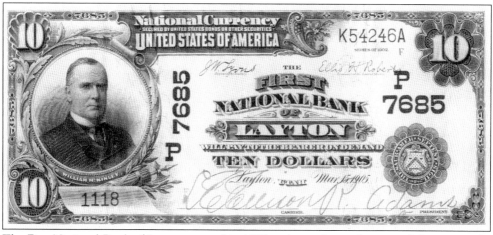

The First National Bank of Layton opened in 1905 and even boasted its own $10 currency for a time. The bank would thrive for more than a century before selling out to Glacier Bancorp of Montana in 2019 to become First Community Bank Utah. At the time of its sale, First National had seven branches and assets of $329 million.

This is the L.S. Heywood Lumber Yard at 24 North Main Street as it looked in approximately 1907. Ellen "Nellie" Heywood, a daughter of the owner, is posing in the picture. The business began in 1904 and sold lumber and farm equipment and also operated a carpenter's shop. It only stayed there until 1910, after which it relocated to 27 East Gentile Street. The building then became a meat shop and was torn down in 1934.

This is the original Layton Drug Store at 11 South Main Street, on the east side of Main Street, which opened in 1910. Robert Birkin was the druggist and handled a wide variety of drugstore items. There was also a telephone switchboard upstairs (staffed by the woman seen in the window). The drugstore moved to 40 North Main Street in 1925, after which several small businesses (a barbershop, bakery, beauty shop, and café) rented the building over the next decade. Rent was just $10 a month. The building was torn down in 1936 to make room for a new service station.

This is another view of the Layton Drug Store as it appeared in the early 1920s. Store manager Robert Birkin is on the left, and an unidentified employee is on the right. The writing in the upper four windows states, "Salt 'em for stock." The store had no connection with the future Layton Drug Store that opened in 1963 as part of the Fort Lane Shopping Center in Layton.

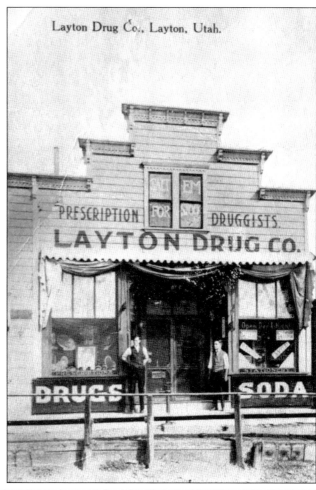

This is a view of Layton's Main Street in about 1912 near the Gentile Street intersection. A horse is towing a broken-down early automobile along a dusty dirt roadway. Note the many horses and wagons still in usage then as well as the presence of telephone/power poles along Main Street. The city's population was less than 500 in that era.

This is the Adams Brothers Meat Market, located at 11 South Main Street. J.I. "Ike" Adams and R.W. "Will" Adams managed the market from 1907 until 1925. Then, Wallace Cowley operated a root beer and ice cream business in the building. The market was torn down in 1936.

This picture shows the havoc of the flooded intersection of Main and Gentile Streets in 1921. This view, looking east, shows how irrigation ditches often overflowed onto the street. Since roads were all dirt in that day, the water caused a muddy mess. Note the horse and wagon, plus the horse to the east of Main Street.

This is the interior of the Stephens-Hennefer Market at 59 West Gentile Street, probably in about 1925. The brick store only operated from 1925 to 1929. Farmer's Union purchased the store's inventory, and Layton City used the building for its offices until 1940. The town post office was also located there, and an addition to the building doubled its size in 1945. The post office relocated to Main Street in 1957.

This picture shows the Adams and Sons General Mercantile Store at 10 North Main Street around the early 1920s. The store was originally called Barton and Company from 1882 until 1890, when George W. Adams and sons Rufus and Marion purchased it. The building burned down in 1892, just a day after its fire insurance policy had expired. Still, it was rebuilt and enlarged and even housed the city's post office until 1915. An undertaker had an office for a time upstairs. The store closed in 1946 and later had many other uses, including being a furniture store, sporting goods outlet, and trading post, before being razed.

Layton City's first fire engine is shown in this photograph from November 1928. That was the year Layton's fire department began, with the engine temporarily housed at Layton Auto's Garage. The first fire station was located at 85 West Gentile Street in 1929. The fire department had eight volunteers at its beginning, and a fire siren was mounted on top of First National Bank to summon the firemen when needed.

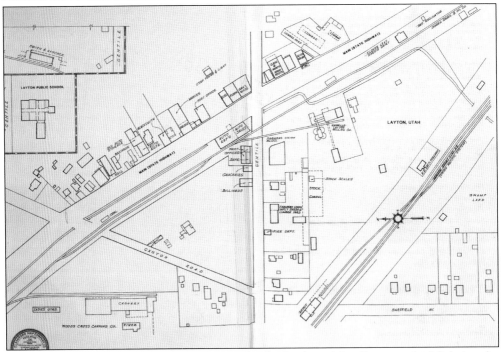

This is a late-1920s map of downtown Layton by the Sanborn Map Company highlighting the city's waterlines and fire protection. Note that the map shows two former street names, Canyon Road and Sheffield Avenue. Canyon Road is now titled Church Street, but the other road no longer exists.

Two

FARMING AND RANCHING

Like most Wasatch Front communities, farming and ranching were a mainstay for early settlers. Club wheat was the first crop likely planted in Layton.

Perhaps the most famous miracle in Utah Pioneer history occurred in June–July 1848, when the first crops in the Salt Lake Valley were threatened by a plague of insects that would later be called "Mormon crickets." Seagulls flew in and eradicated the pests.

The Layton area may have experienced its own farming miracle six years later. During the summer of 1854, grasshoppers threatened to destroy all the crops of settlers in the Layton-Kaysville area. This insect horde rose one morning like a low, dark cloud. However, huge wind gusts soon came from the eastern canyons and carried the grasshoppers out over the Great Salt Lake.

Millions of dead insects later washed up on the shores of the lake, and most of the settlers' crops were spared.

However, a lack of summer water was the perennial problem for Layton farmers. Some of the first dry farming in the nation happened on the north end of Layton City. The Holmes Creek Dam was first built in 1852 to store water for settlers in the Layton area. This was also the oldest dam in Utah and one of the first in the western United States. However, the drought of 1855–1856 was so hard on crops that Layton-area settlers were forced to eat sego lily plants and wild onions to survive.

The completion of the Davis and Weber Canal in 1885 and the opening of East Canyon Reservoir in 1899 equaled reliable water distribution and supply for farmers.

Commercial farming was underway by 1900 in Layton, when alfalfa became a very common crop, along with grains, tomatoes, onions, peas, and sugar beets. Large cattle herds were not common, but a railcar of cattle, about 30, was an average among farmers.

Layton used to have some large stockyards on the south end of town, just west of Main Street. Layton was then reported to be one of the most important cattle shipping points in the state, with 5,000 cattle being fed and shipped from the Layton stockyards each year.

An unidentified large Layton family poses for a picture after delivering harvested produce, possibly tomatoes, to the Layton Canning Company at 80 North Cross Street around 1906. Layton Canning began business in 1903. Its wooden warehouse (shown here) was blown down in 1906 and replaced with a brick structure. The company merged with the Wood Cross Canning Company in 1913. The company's factory was torn down in 1954, but the warehouse remained and was remodeled as a recreation center for the original St. Rose of Lima Catholic Church.

This 1912 winter-time photograph, taken from the top of the Farmer's Union Building at 12 South Main Street looking northeast, shows the large open farm fields around what would become Layton's historic main business street. The railroad depot is on the lower left-hand side. The Adams and Sons Store at 10 North Main Street is the large building on the right-hand side.

Layton farm workers are shown sharing a drink from a water bucket in a sugar beet field, probably in west Layton during the 1920s. The men were likely topping the beets. The tops were left in the field, and sheep would be herded in to eat the toppings in the fall after the beets were harvested.

The Harris Dairy Company was a short-lived business in Layton during the 1920s. Its truck is shown in front of the Farmer's Union Building, though the dairy was located farther south on Main Street. Layton boasted several other dairy businesses in the past, including Layton Dairy and Queen Dairy.

Layton rancher Blaine Adams herds his sheep westwards down Gentile Street from his pastures above Fort Lane to some grazing land near the Del Adams home in west Layton. This late-1930s picture highlights Layton's former agricultural heritage, not only of farm fields but also of ranching.

Edgar Adams shows off his horse in an undated Layton ranching picture, probably from the early 1910s. Adams had a large sheep ranch in town. However, sheep were not common among Layton's 19th-century households. Estimates are that only 15 percent of early farms included sheep. The area's largest sheep ranch was on Antelope Island, where up to 8,000 sheep roamed. Christopher Layton, the city's namesake, tended those sheep for five years during his early career in Davis County. (Courtesy of Harris Adams.)

Three

SUGAR FACTORY

Early Layton had more than agriculture going—it had some large industries in town. The Layton Milling Company was the state's top-producing flour mill in 1903. By 1913, Layton had sugar beets on 700 acres. However, they had to be shipped to a factory in Lehi, Utah, for processing, and an extra shipping charge made farmers increasingly unhappy. That's why the Layton Sugar Company started in 1915.

The Layton plant was built on 60 acres of land formerly owned by J.H. Layton and Harriet E. Ellison. Construction began in March 1915 and was completed by early October of that year. The factory had access to a new spur line of the Oregon Short Line Railroad.

The facility was originally built to produce and house up to 110,000 bags of sugar extracted from sugar beets.

James Layton, a former mayor of Layton, grew up in west Layton, near the warehouse.

"There's a lot of stories about that place," he said, referring to tales like children being sewn inside 100-pound sacks and left for several hours as pranks.

According to Kent Day, a Layton historian, two generations of Layton residents grew accustomed to the sights, sounds, and smells of Layton's sugar factory. The black smoke of the factory, the 4:00 p.m. whistle at the end of the workday, and wagonloads of beets on Gentile Street are things Layton residents do not experience anymore.

"But hardly anyone longs for a whiff of beet pulp from boots sitting next to the kitchen stove," he wrote in his history of Layton's sugar beet industry.

In fact, the sugar beet industry was so brisk in 1918 that a hotel was actually built about 400 feet west of Sugar Street to house sugar factory workers.

After the war, housing continued to increase, and that, coupled with more farmers taking jobs at Hill Air Force Base and more imported sugar cane, led to the closure of the factory in 1963. Much of the factory was torn down in 1972, and the rest followed in 2001.

This is a sack of sugar produced from sugar beets at the Layton Sugar Factory. Bags of sugar were sold locally at the Layton Farmer's Union store. In the 1917–1918 growing season, the factory paid Layton farmers a total of $300,000 for their sugar beet crops, and while the plant was in business, many Layton farmers grew sugar beets.

The Layton Sugar Factory opened in 1915 and was located just northwest of where today's Smith's Layton Distribution Plant is found. It meant local farmers did not have to send their beets to a plant in Lehi, Utah, more than 100 miles away. The only year the plant did not operate was 1934, when a terrible drought devastated farmers.

The Layton Sugar Factory survived through the Great Depression. However, nearly all World War II–era construction in Layton was done on farmland. This pattern eventually downsized the yield of the sugar factory. Also, some farmers gained employment at Hill Air Force Base, and that equaled less farms being worked.

A Layton farmer dumps a load of harvested sugar beets onto a conveyor belt at the Layton Sugar Factory, probably in the 1920s. It required a team of horses to haul and dump the heavy load.

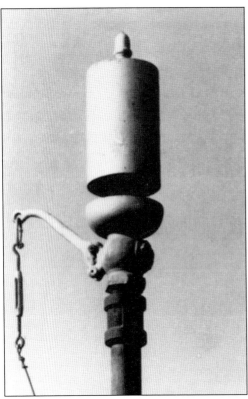

This is the huge whistle that sat atop the Layton Sugar Factory. It was audible over most of Layton City. The three daily whistles, at 8:00 a.m., noon, and 4:00 p.m., were a standard "clock setter" for much of the city for almost five decades, from 1915 until 1963.

This unidentified young Layton girl is dwarfed standing in front of a huge pile of sugar beets near the Layton Sugar Factory, probably in the 1930s. These beets put a huge demand on soil nutrients and required farmers to use fertilizers when they planted this same crop on land year after year. Production of refined sugar from Utah sugar beets was encouraged by Brigham Young as early as 1850. However, it took 36 years of trial and error among Utah farmers to yield significant crops of beets.

The Layton Sugar Factory is seen here from the west side. By the 1950s, the population of Layton had increased so much and the employment opportunities were so diverse that the sugar factory no longer had much of an economic impact on Layton City.

This is the backside of the Layton Sugar Factory Warehouse, located just west of where today's Smith's Food Plant is. The large warehouse had direct access to the railroad and was torn down in 2001 after years of abandonment. Today, the only reminder of the once-thriving industry is the Sugar Street name.

This is an aerial view of Layton City in 1939 centered on Main and Gentile Streets. The picture was taken by Frank Adams as he flew from Ogden to Salt Lake. The Layton Sugar Factory is just out of sight on the far left. The Oregon Short Line Railroad station is in the lower left corner, and the "White Chapel" of the Church of Jesus Christ of Latter-day Saints, on Gentile Street, is in the upper right corner. The city's business district is in the center of the picture.

The demolition of the Layton Sugar Factory took place in 1972, a total of 57 years after it was constructed. The factory was Layton's tallest building for many years. The facility's warehouse remained for another 29 years before it was also razed in 2001. An industrial park now resides on the property.

Four

TRANSPORTATION

A horse or wagon ride to Salt Lake or Ogden from Layton usually required half a day or more in Layton's early decades. However, by the late 19th century, three major railroads rolled through Layton. The Oregon Short Line ran directly through downtown, and the Denver & Rio Grande line was to the west. In addition, the Bamberger Railroad was located where Interstate 15 is now.

The poor condition of roads was a big issue back in the 1910s for Layton. "Road from Ogden to Salt Lake a disgrace" was a March 3, 1918, headline in the *Ogden Standard-Examiner*. "Automobiles sink eighteen inches into the soft mud and cannot be pulled out—Truck now stuck in the mud," the article stated.

Hill Air Force Base in the 1940s increased Layton road expansion. In the summer of 1952, Layton City experienced one of its first residential traffic jams, caused by the many commuters leaving Hill Air Force Base. In 1953–1954, a four-lane highway was finally opened all the way from Brigham City to Provo.

When an interstate highway was proposed to go through Davis County in the early 1960s, Highway 89 was Ogden City's preferred route, since it offered the best access, to Utah's second-largest city. That was eliminated by the federal government because a route to the west offered better access to all the government facilities in the area.

After three years of work, Interstate 15 from south Layton to Ogden opened on November 23, 1966, in what could only be described as a blockbuster moment in the city's history. This instantly meant Main Street (Highway 91) would no longer be so congested with commuters during shift changes at Hill Air Force Base. (Some 15,000 workers were employed at Hill AFB back then.) And decades later, the proximity to Interstate 15 helped create the Layton Hills Mall, which in turn attracted an entire retail and restaurant area just east of the freeway.

The final completion of the freeway in Davis County was the stretch from South Layton to Farmington. That was not done until 1977 because of several complicated land issues.

This is the Oregon Short Line Railroad station as it looked in the early 1900s. It was built in 1892 at 23 North Main Street. The railroad constructed a larger station at 160 West Gentile Street in 1912 beside a new double-track line.

This picture is a back street view of Main Street shops looking north about 1905. It shows the rear of businesses on the west side of Main Street, with Gentile Street—and a horse and wagon—crossing in the center. The original Short Line Railroad depot is in the center of the picture. The large building in the distance to the left is the Layton Canning Company warehouse.

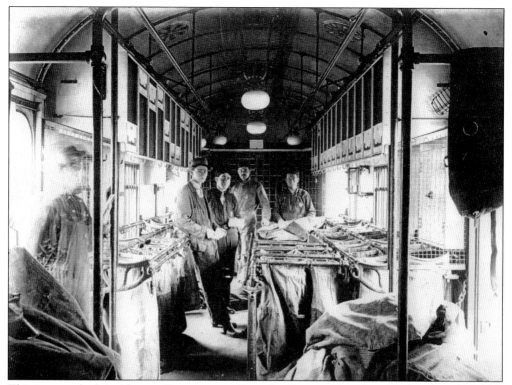

This is a rare look inside a mail sorting car along the Oregon Short Line Railroad in 1907. The train is making a run from Salt Lake City to Butte, Montana. Jessie Harris, a Layton resident and US Post Office employee, is at the far right in the picture. To save time, workers actually sorted mail as the train moved along between towns. (Courtesy of Harris Adams.)

This is one of the only photographs known to exist of the Bamberger Railroad station in Layton. The Bamberger was primarily a passenger service that linked Salt Lake and Ogden and in between. The Layton station opened in 1912, though the Bamberger line reached Layton in 1906. The Bamberger line had its last run on September 6, 1952. Today's Interstate 15 follows much of the path of the former railroad line. (Courtesy of Harris Adams.)

This picture shows an early motorized hearse in Layton for the funeral of William C. Layton, who was killed on July 23, 1918, in a railroad accident in France during World War I. The hearse is waiting for Layton's body to arrive at the Layton train station. (Courtesy of Harris Adams.)

Motorcycles were very popular in the early 20th century. Shown here are six Layton men posing with their cycles in a 1917 photograph of their motorcycle club on the south side of the Adams Store at 10 Main Street, just north of Gentile Street. Dr. Walter Whitlock is believed to have organized this motorcycle club in Layton.

This is a Harley-Davidson motorcycle sleigh in Layton, probably in a winter of the 1920s. Bill Day is likely the passenger on the right side, while the other two men are unidentified. The "snow cycle" is in front of the Ernest Layton Auto Repair Shop at 33 South Main Street. Spectators watch the curious vehicle from the north on the front steps of Ernest Layton Hardware Store at 27 South Main Street.

This picture shows the highway just north of Layton, which was the main artery between Salt Lake and Ogden, on August 9, 1920. This road was known in that era as Highway 91 (and Main Street in Layton) but was later renamed U-126. It was paved with concrete in the 1920s yet had no striping and was still lightly traveled, with only one vehicle showing in the picture. Note the many trees along the highway.

This picture, taken looking northwest, highlights severe flooding along the Layton rail depot in a wet spring of the 1920s. A culvert under Gentile Street would often plug up with debris and flood portions of South Main Street. As a train passes by, workers contemplate how to best manage the water flow.

A Ford Model T car rolls along Layton's unpaved Main Street in this c. 1920 picture. Bill Day, on the left, is the passenger, while the driver is unidentified. The car is heading south in front of the Ernest Layton Building, located at 27 South Main. The building included a hardware store on the first floor and a hotel and café on the second floor.

This is Layton's Main Street looking north as it appeared in the late 1920s. Main Street was a narrow concrete highway, and there were no sidewalks at that time. Businesses only had limited wooden boardwalks in front of their properties. The Adams and Sons store at 16 North Main Street also housed Davis County Furniture (later renamed Union Furniture).

This is how Layton's main business district appeared in 1961. This view was taken looking south on Main Street towards Gentile Street, where the city's first traffic signal was installed during World War II. Note the wide, four-lane divided highway with numerous streetlights above the roadway. In fact, Main Street had so many streetlights in the area that the city council soon decided to remove some of the lights, as the city's electric bill had skyrocketed.

Five

WORLD WAR II AND HILL AIR FORCE BASE

Perhaps the most pivotal date in all of Layton City history was December 7, 1941. The Japanese attack on Pearl Harbor and the United States' entry into World War II changed Layton and the surrounding area forever.

Hill Field was already under construction in 1940, but World War II escalated progress and activity at military bases in the area, and Layton's population soared. In 1940, Layton was a small, sleepy farming town with a population of just 646 people.

"It was kind of a closed group," Jay Dansie, a lifelong Layton resident, recalled during a 2014 interview about life in Layton before Hill came along. "It was still a settlement of families," he noted, explaining that there just were not many outsiders. That all changed, Dansie said, when Verdeland Park, a massive World War II military housing development, opened in 1943 where Layton High School, the Layton city offices, and Commons Park are today. It boasted some 1,500 residents—half the city's population—in its heyday.

"The whole city changed when Verdeland Park went in," Dansie said. "It changed the city forever."

Indeed, Main Street was widened. The city's first traffic signal went in during 1943 at Main and Gentile Streets, as Layton's population had multiplied.

At the time Verdeland Park was built, Layton City had a population of about 960 citizens. By the end of 1943, about 1,440 residents were living in Verdeland Park, thus more than doubling the population of Layton City.

Residents of Verdeland Park worked at Hill Field and the Navy Supply Depot, and since many of the heads of the households were serving in the military, a lot of the workers who lived in Verdeland Park were women.

The year 1944 represented a milestone for Layton City, as the community coped with an increasing population from Hill Air Force Base personnel and families during World War II. By 1950, Layton's population had increased more than five-fold to 3,456.

This is the official ground breaking at Hill Field on January 12, 1940, in a blizzard that was part of the wettest northern Utah winter since 1890. A 75-auto caravan braved the slippery roads for the ceremony, and only the War Department's heavy equipment made the route passable. Hill's main gate is on the Layton side of the base. Hill Air Force Base is situated on a hill above much of Layton City, but the base was actually named after Maj. Ployer P. Hill of the US Army Air Corps, who perished while test-flying a prototype of the B-17 bomber. (Courtesy of Utah State Historical Society.)

Cement work on a Hill Field runway is shown in an August 20, 1940, picture. Although grading on the base's four runways had begun in November 1938, they were not paved until the summer of 1940 and not completed until September 1, 1941, at a huge cost of $1.35 million. The runways were 7,500 feet long and 150 feet wide. (Courtesy of Utah State Historical Society.)

GROUND BREAKING, HILL FIELD, 12 JAN 1940

This September 1940 photograph by the *Salt Lake Tribune* shows Hangar No. 1 at Hill Field under construction. Work on the operations hangar and annexes began on July 24, 1940, and was not completed until October 17, 1941, at a cost of $503,728. (Courtesy of Utah State Historical Society.)

The attack on Pearl Harbor on December 7, 1941, forever changed Layton City and northern Davis County, as the area became a military focal point. The *Honolulu Star-Bulletin* newspaper was one of the first papers to report on the Japanese surprise attack.

This picture shows two young Japanese students at Layton Elementary School posing on the school grounds, probably in the late 1930s. Because of its many farms, Layton had a significant Japanese population when World War II began. Some young men in Layton Japanese families served in the US military during the war, but some anti-Japanese sentiment was still prevalent during wartime.

This picture shows Verdeland Park. The US government condemned 85 acres of land owned by six Layton families and bought it for $23,934 on May 12, 1942, to establish an area for Verdeland Park housing. Renters were accepted in January 1943 for almost 400 units. To qualify, one or both heads of a household had to work at Hill Field. The housing units were made of plywood and had a living room and one, two, or three bedrooms, with rent being $21.50, $24.50, or $31.50 respectively per month. The houses were laid out in sections, with an alphabetical listing of A to P.

This is a mid-1940s picture of six Layton men and two officers at a Layton military recruitment center. The third man from the left is Wally Nalder, while the fourth from the left is Devon Day. The other four young men and officers are unidentified. Military enlistment remained a popular venture, even after World War II had ended.

This is a May 1948 aerial photograph of Hill Air Force Base showing the extensive development of the facility since its beginnings almost a decade earlier. Note the large number of aircraft, in storage following World War II, at the top of the picture. Hill Air Force Base was originally named Hill Field from 1940 to 1948, until the transition to the new US Air Force away from the former US Army Air Force. (Courtesy of Utah State Historical Society.)

This 1948 photograph shows a group of the many airplanes stored east of Hill Field's runways after World War II. An estimated 700 aircraft, mostly B-26s, were mothballed, but there were 144 B-29 Superfortresses stored at Hill AFB too after the war. (Courtesy of Utah State Historical Society.)

Six

SCHOOLS AND CHURCHES

Layton had eight or more one-room schoolhouses scattered about town in the late 19th century. On October 12, 1902, Layton Elementary School opened at 339 West Gentile Street and consolidated them. The original Layton Elementary School was torn down in 1984 and replaced with a modern building.

Central Davis Junior High School in Layton was not always known as such. It was originally titled Layton Junior High School. The school was dedicated on January 24, 1955. (By the time North Layton Junior High School opened in the 1970s, Layton Junior was retitled Central Davis.)

Davis High in Kaysville opened in 1914, and Layton residents attended there until Layton High began in 1966.

The demise of Verdeland Park opened the door to the development of Layton High School on its former land. Northridge High School, Layton's second high school, began in 1992.

As of 2019, Layton has a total of 18 public schools in its boundaries, plus some academies and private schools.

Weber State University opened its Davis County satellite campus at a permanent location in Layton in 2003.

Being a pioneer community, first settled by members of the Church of Jesus Christ of Latter-day Saints, means that it is still Layton's predominant religion.

Layton Latter-day Saints were part of Kaysville wards for more than 40 years. Layton's first ward came along in 1892. It was a frame building near 367 East 1000 North.

The Episcopalian Church was the first non-LDS faith in town, with St. Jude's Church and School that began in 1888 at 319 West Gentile Street. It eventually moved to Main Street and closed in 1916, because of low attendance.

Prior to World War II, there were few non-Latter-day Saint families living in Layton or even Davis County. The war changed that.

St. Rose of Lima Catholic Church, located at the west corner of Main and Church Streets, was dedicated on April 11, 1948. Catholicism had become Utah's second-largest religion, and Layton was no exception. That building was replaced in 1995 by a larger St. Rose of Lima Church at 210 Chapel Street.

As of 2019, Layton had 19 non-LDS churches in its boundaries.

This was the one-room Five Points school, located at the intersection of Main Street, Fort Lane, and Rosewood Lane. A.B. Cook was one of the school's first teachers. Every day, he walked from South Weber to the school. The school closed in 1902 when Layton Elementary School opened on West Gentile Street.

This custom-made school bus was driven in 1925 by Robert E. Green of Layton to deliver students from West Layton to Layton Elementary School. Green, who drove school buses for 37 years, began in 1922 by driving a horse-drawn sheep wagon as a makeshift school bus. His specially made 1925 bus was constructed in Ogden. Green made $60 a month driving school buses but had to pay for his own gasoline. He said students sometimes got into fights on the bus. He once even caught students playing cards and getting ready to make bets at the rear of the bus.

Layton Elementary School is pictured as it appeared new in the early 20th century. The school opened on October 12, 1902, with Joseph A. Sill as principal. The building cost just over $4,000 to construct on West Gentile Street. It was expanded to an eight-room school in 1915. A cafeteria was added in 1950.

This is a sweeping view of a fifth- or sixth-grade class at Layton Elementary School during the 1920s. Roy Ole Layton is the teacher of the class. Layton, from Kaysville, taught at the school for many years. He died in 1945 at age 48. Note that the majority of the students in the photograph have their arms neatly folded.

Some Layton Elementary students pose for a picture while working on a first-aid course at school. This is probably in the mid-1930s and is in the school's gymnasium, which was on the second floor. Roy Ole Layton is the teacher for the unidentified students. Other teachers at Layton Elementary in the 1930s include Blanche Adams, Sarah J. Adams, Vilato Aplanap, Mary P. Ware, Nora Blood, Kristie Bodily, Ima B. Whitesides, Mary Briggs, Edith Nelson, Muruel Reeves, Rita Wilson, Olive Castro, George S. Cooper, and Irma Hyde.

This is another Layton Elementary School classroom scene, probably from the 1930s. The students are all coloring drawings in the class. There are also several Red Cross posters on the wall in the classroom. Elijah George "E.G." King was the principal and a teacher at Layton Elementary for many years. A future Layton elementary school, E.G. King, located at 601 East 1000 North, was named in his honor. King died in 1967 at age 86.

A group of seventh- or eighth-grade students are shown exercising on the field behind Layton Elementary School, probably in the 1930s. The seventh and eighth grades attended Layton Elementary School until junior high schools began in Davis County. Note that girls in dresses were doing the same exercises as the boys.

Two rows of boys and two rows of girls are shown neatly line up for exercise routines on the ball field behind Layton Elementary School. These seventh- or eighth-graders are likely pictured in the 1930s. Note the ethnic diversity among the students. Also, the Ella Dawson home and barn are clearly visible in the background.

Layton Elementary School, located at 369 West Gentile Street, is seen here as it appeared in the early 1980s. The school was built in 1902 and expanded over the decades. The current modern Layton Elementary opened in 1984 and replaced the original structure, which was torn down. In the school's early decades, students walking to class had to tramp through deep mud or dusty roads unless they got a ride on a wagon or bobsleigh.

This is an early picture of Central Davis Junior High School at 663 North Church Street, back when it was known as Layton Junior High School. The school first opened in 1955. Students used the armory next door for their gymnasium. A much larger shared gym, a collaborative effort between the Davis School District and Layton City, opened in 2002.

This is an aerial view, probably in the late 1960s, of the Layton High School campus on Wasatch Drive, east of Commons Park. Layton High swung open its doors to students in the fall of 1966, providing a local high school that Layton students could attend instead of having to travel to Davis High School in Kaysville. Note the small number of cars in the parking lot. Layton High is located where Verdeland Park, a government housing unit, was situated until 1962.

Northridge was the second high school to open in Layton and the seventh high school in Davis County. Classes there began in the fall of 1992 at 2430 North Hill Field Road. The school cost $28.6 million and sits on 47 acres of land. The property before the school was built was undeveloped and was purchased for $1 million by the Davis School District. The nickname of the school is the "Ridge," and the mascot is the Knights.

This is the Weber State University Davis Campus, located just south of U-193 in Layton. Weber State University opened its original Davis Center at Layton in the former Mountain Fuel building on Gordon Avenue in 1997. Weber premiered the first of 10 proposed buildings on a full-service campus, located at 2750 University Park Boulevard, in 2003—and is still expanding. (Author photograph.)

Gentile Street, pictured on this street sign, is perhaps the most unusually named street in all of Layton. By the most accepted tale, the street was named for the Gentiles (non-members of the Church of Jesus Christ of Latter-day Saints) who lived west of Main Street in the late 19th century. By another version, the families living there included "Jack Mormons" (inactive Latter-day Saints). By still another version, the road led west to Bluff Road, which was a popular emigrant route for non-Mormon travelers through the area. Several Latter-day Saint chapels line Gentile Street today, and there is also a Kingdom Hall of the Jehovah's Witnesses along the road. (Author photograph.)

This is the original West Layton Latter-day Saint Ward Chapel on West Gentile Street. It was dedicated in 1901 by church president Joseph F. Smith and cost $5,600 plus labor. An addition to the building, with classrooms and amusement hall, was started in 1927 and dedicated in 1936. This building was torn down in 1971 and was replaced by a new chapel at 2120 West Gentile Street, just west of the original church.

Three young Layton boys and their horse are show surveying the extensive damage to the Layton Latter-day Saint Ward Chapel at 367 East 1000 North. Lightning and a fire destroyed the church building on July 24, 1936. This $11,210 brick chapel had been in use since 1908. The ward members had already outgrown the facility, and plans had been started a year prior to replace the chapel with a larger one.

The Layton White Chapel of the Church of Jesus Christ of Latter-day Saints is pictured in 1939. This meetinghouse was built in 1937 at 195 East Gentile Street. It was dedicated by church president Heber J. Grant. This church replaced a chapel on 1000 North that was destroyed by a lightning-caused fire in 1936. This church also featured the first full-size basketball court of any ward in the entire church. A portion of the old chapel is used as business offices today.

The West Layton Latter-day Saint Ward Chapel, near 2100 West Gentile Street, shows the addition to the original chapel on the right side. The expanded buildings were started in 1927 and completed in 1936. Members donated money, goods, and labor over nearly a decade-long period—during the Great Depression—to complete the building additions, which included classrooms and an amusement hall. A three-act play and a community dance were held in the new hall to celebrate the completion. Pres. David O. McKay, from the first presidency, dedicated the new facilities on February 23, 1936. (Courtesy of Utah State Historical Society.)

The Wat Dhammagunara Buddhist Temple, located at 644 East 1000 North, opened in 1975 and, prior to the announcement in 2018 of the Layton Latter-day Saint Temple coming to Layton, was the only "temple" in town. The congregation was started by emigrants from Thailand, most of whom came to Utah in the 1970s. Many were the wives of American servicemen, especially airmen from Hill Air Force Base. (Author photograph.)

The modern St. Rose of Lima Catholic Church is shown here. It opened in 1994 at 210 South Chapel Street. Its cross rises 117 feet above the street level, and the church includes 18,000 square feet. This building replaced the original Layton Catholic church, at the corner of Main and Church Streets. That St. Rose of Lima chapel began services in 1948 and was replaced by the Chapel Street facility. The original version was sold by the Catholic Church in 1995 and had other uses, such as a restaurant. It was torn down in 2015 to make way for new town homes. (Author photograph.)

This open farm field is the site of a new temple for the Church of Jesus Christ of Latter-day Saints in Layton. Announced in 2018, the structure is located south of Oak Hills Drive and east of Rosewood Lane. This medium-sized temple is located on land primarily used for farming, which dates back to the 1850s. (Author photograph.)

This is an artist's exterior rendering of the new Layton, Utah, Temple of the Church of Jesus Christ of Latter-day Saints. This temple will be located at the corner of Oak Hills Drive and Rosewood Lane, and plans call for a three-story temple of approximately 87,000 square feet. This will be the second temple in Davis County, with the first being the Bountiful Temple, which opened in 1995. (Courtesy of the Church of Jesus Christ of Latter-day Saints.)

Seven

COMMUNITY LIFE

Webster's Grove, a large patch of trees planted by George W. Webster on Angel Street in Kaysville, was the first widespread recreation spot for Layton. Its heyday was the early 1880s to the turn of the century, and it had swings, baseball fields, and even a dance hall.

Early Layton residents also often went to the short-lived Lake Side resort, located southwest of Kaysville. It opened in 1870, offering a chance to "float like a cork" in the Great Salt Lake. By 1886, Lagoon was also a popular resort for Laytonites (and still is today).

The Hillbilly Band, Webster's Grove and Pavilion, Kaysville Opera House, Layton Opera House, Kaysville Brass Band, and Fiddler's Creek are all entertainment-based features from Layton's past.

The first official sporting event inside today's boundaries of Layton City recorded in a newspaper was a baseball game between the unincorporated community of Layton and Kaysville residents. The game was played in Layton on Decoration Day, May 30, 1901, according to the *Davis County Clipper* newspaper of June 7, 1901. Layton defeated Kaysville 2-0 in a morning contest on the diamond, and then it also blanked a team from South Weber 2-0 in an afternoon contest.

Layton City's first theater was the La'Tonia (also called "La Tonia"), on North Main Street. It opened in 1914 and featured silent movies at first, with live accompaniment.

On August 27, 1957, Layton City paid the federal government $580,000 for the 72-acre Verdeland Park land. That led to Commons Park. Layton now has more than a dozen parks and many trails.

The Fernwood picnic area first opened in 1959. It was built in an area that was originally known as Fernwood Flats.

Ground was broken for the Valley View Golf Course, located at 2501 East Gentile Street, back in 1972. Layton City bought the land for the course, and Davis County developed the facility. Layton's second golf course, Sun Hills, at 1250 East 3185 North, opened in the late summer of 1995. The Swan Lakes Golf Course opened in 1993 and closed after the 2019 season to become a residential development.

The John Henry Layton family stands in front of their large home at 683 West Gentile Street in West Layton. The photograph was taken between 1885 and 1897, before Layton had separated from Kaysville and decades before Layton was its own official town. The house was considered a "high style" home for its time, with elements of a Queen Anne style. The home has been added to the National Register of Historic Places. It is now owned by Layton mayor Joy Petro. She is Layton's first female mayor and has lived in the historic home for more than 28 years. (Courtesy of the Utah State Historical Society.)

The Layton Roller Mills entry is shown in the July 24, 1897, Pioneer Parade in Salt Lake City, having just passed by the Brigham Young Monument. This event highlighted the Pioneer Semi-Centennial. Since Layton was not yet a city, the float also highlights Davis County. A flour mill, the business began in 1890 in Layton at 36 South Main Street. Note the many trolley cars in the background of the picture. In 14 more years (1911), the Hotel Utah (today's Joseph Smith Memorial Building) would fill the corner on the right side of the parade.

Basketball was initially more popular with women than men in its early years. This 1912 Layton team of young women was sponsored by the Layton Latter-day Saint Ward. The team won all five games it played that year, including against Kaysville High School. From left to right, the players are Vera Morgan Adams, Alta Craig Ronnencamp, Luella Nalder Rosemait, Lou Morgan Spackman, an unidentified teacher from Layton Elementary, Nellie Adams Sanders, Ramona Whitesides Hill, and Lillie Young Dawson.

The John A. Layton family of Layton poses for a Democratic Party event at Lagoon Park, Farmington, in the summer of 1914. Lagoon was a popular summer outing for Layton residents from when it opened in 1886 to today. The park initially offered just a lake, shade, and games, eventually adding amusement park rides, like a carousel and a roller coaster, and much more over the decades. (Courtesy of Harris Adams.)

Layton Elementary School also sponsored football teams for its younger students. This unspecified picture appears to be fifth- or sixth-graders in the late 1920s. Note that the players are only wearing leather helmets. Numerous injuries and even some fatalities nationwide from playing football was a big controversy at the time, mainly due to inadequate safety equipment.

A trio of Layton Boy Scouts marches in an unidentified parade in town, possibly in the 1920s. Two young girls are also sitting on the bumper of a decorated car. It could have been a military parade relating to World War I.

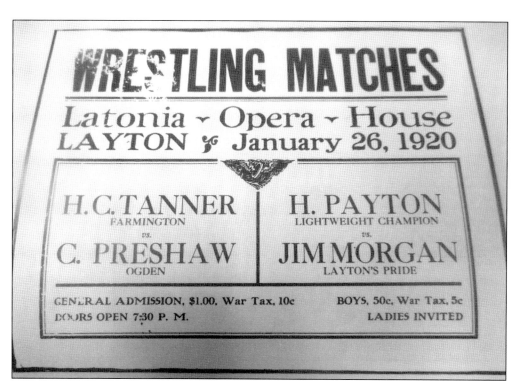

WRESTLING MATCHES
Latonia ⚘ Opera ⚘ House
LAYTON ⚘ January 26, 1920

H. C. TANNER	H. PAYTON
FARMINGTON	LIGHTWEIGHT CHAMPION
vs.	vs.
C. PRESHAW	JIM MORGAN
OGDEN	LAYTON'S PRIDE

GENERAL ADMISSION, $1.00, War Tax, 10c   BOYS, 50c, War Tax, 5c
DOORS OPEN 7:30 P. M.   LADIES INVITED

This January 26, 1920, poster illustrates the popularity of the sport of wrestling in the 1920s. Jim Morgan of Layton was one of the featured wrestlers in the matches. At $1 for adult admission, that equals more than $13 in today's dollar value. Also note that there was a war tax of 5¢ or 10¢ added onto admission costs. Note too that ladies were especially invited to attend the wrestling event.

W.W. "Blacky" Garrett was a third baseman for the Layton Baseball team, probably in the 1930s. Baseball was likely the most popular sport in Layton during the first half of the 20th century. Basketball, football, and soccer were also popular sports by the end of the century. (Courtesy of Harris Adams.)

A baseball team from Layton is shown here around 1930. The photograph was taken at Lagoon Park, a popular hot spot for baseball games in that era. From left to right are (first row) Reed Simmons, Samuel Scoffield, Kenneth Page, Lewis Major, Ural Major, and Stanford Cowley; (second row) Clair Whitesides, Norman Brown, John Brown, Ted Brown, Kenneth Slater, Bill Cowley, Lewis Briggs, Robert Barton, and Fred Jones. The photographer was Lewis Major.

The Layton Elementary football team in the mid-1930s is pictured. Elementary schools in Davis County sponsored grid teams in the era before junior high schools came along. Note the leather helmets and the cloth shoulder pads.

Elizabeth Adams and Rufus "Will" Adams stand in front of their home at 144 East 2000 North (today's Antelope Drive) in 1940. Will was a Davis County School Board member and built the home in 1910. The home was recently remodeled, and today, some of the Adams family still live in the house.

The American Legion Post 87 is shown here, located in Layton at 128 South Main Street. Built in a log cabin style, the American Legion building opened in Layton in November 1942. The group is a social and mutual-aid veterans' organization, including members of the US armed forces. A historical marker affixed to a large rock on the Legion property commemorates where Layton's stagecoach stop used to be. Christopher Layton built the Prairie House in 1858 near the stop to cater to stagecoach passengers.

Horses, like those shown here, were still a popular fixture among longtime Layton families in the 1940s. This 1943 picture was taken in Hobbs Hollow. Some of the riders include Mike Adams, Lyle Porter, Neil Adams, and Paul Adams. Don Evans is sitting on the ground. Gwen Porter's automobile is on the left side. (Courtesy of Harris Adams.)

This is the Flint stable building, located at 160 North Flint Street. Leland Flint of Layton constructed the facility for horse training, a hobby of his. His family name became the title of the street too. Since 1996, Saltaire Farms has used the property as a popular equestrian center.

This is a copy of the cover of the souvenir program on Layton City's first Riata Days over the Fourth of July holiday in 1948. *Riata* means a long looped rope to catch animals and was intended to honor Layton's ranching and agricultural heritage. The Riata name lasted more than 40 years, with its last usage in 1990. Beginning in 1991, Liberty Days became Layton's title for its Fourth of July festivities. The name was chosen from a contest to rename the event.

SOUVENIR PROGRAM
Layton Riata Days
JULY 2 - 3 - 4 - 5, 1948

25c

This is the Stott Brothers Welding float in the July 4, 1948, Riata Days Parade in Layton. The float, which focuses on liberty and freedom, also highlights that a mainstay of the Stott Brothers' business is fixing radiators.

This is a 1940s flyer announcing the dedication of the new Layton City Hall at 37 East Gentile Street. A dedication ceremony on September 27, 1940, was held for the new building. A renovation was made at the old city hall in 1953 to accommodate the fire department. A new fire station, still in use, was built in 1972 at 199 North Fort Lane.

The Layton Town Board Is Pleased to Invite the Public to the

Dedication

of the

Layton Town Hall

Layton Town's New Municipal Building

Friday, September 27, 1940
8:00 P. M.

This is the First National Bank of Layton float in the Riata Days Parade, probably in the early 1950s. The float is headed west down Gentile Street and is passing by the Farmer's Union store. Since the Farmer's Union closed in 1957, this means this parade took place before that. Early Layton Fourth of July parades used to end at Layton Elementary School.

This is a Layton Riata Days Parade float from the early 1950s. The eight children on the float may be part of St. Rose of Lima Catholic Church, since the center child in the elevated chair appears to have wings on her back. The original St. Rose of Lima Catholic Church in Layton was located near the west intersection of Main and Church Streets. This church was dedicated on April 11, 1948.

Judith Adams, right, daughter of Harris and Ethel Adams, sits atop a float in the Riata Days Parade of July 4, 1952, flanked by other Layton children. The float is in front of Layton Cold Storage and Grocery Store at 156 West Gentile Street. Note the reference on the store to S&H Green Stamps, which were popular in that era but were discontinued by the late 1980s.

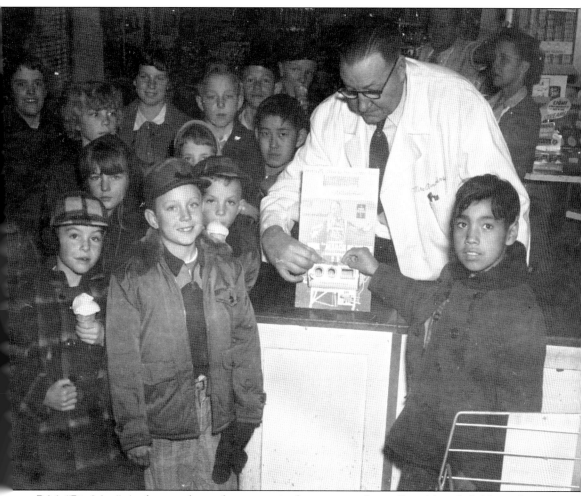

B.M. "Big Man" Anderson, shown here, was six feet, nine inches tall and loved children. As the owner of Layton Cold Storage at 156 West Gentile Street, located near Layton Elementary School, he sponsored periodic contests for children, like this one. He opened his business in 1944 and later added a grocery store in the front section. He joked to kids that he was only "five feet, twenty-one inches" tall. Anderson was also a member of the Layton Town Board in the late 1940s (pre–city council era).

Wayne Winegar, owner of Wayne's Food Town Store, presents flowers to Miss Davis County at the grand opening of his new building near Fort Lane and Gentile Street in the mid-1950s. A helicopter pilot flew VIPs in for the event. Winegar was the mayor of Layton from 1958 to 1960. He also leased his Layton grocery store to Smith's Food Town in 1960.

These were Layton's National Guard Queens for 1957, named in February of that year. From left to right are Calene Henrie, Pat Furman, Judy Sartor, and Dixie Gittins. The year 1957 was also when construction began on the Layton Armory, just west of Central Davis Junior High School. When the armory opened in January 1958, the $230,000 facility provided extra classrooms and a new gymnasium for an overcrowded school next door.

This is a large crowd of excited children and parents converging in the parking lot of the new Fort Lane Shopping Center to await the annual arrival of Santa Claus in the mid-1960s. Hosted by area store merchants, children received candy from Santa, and the event just after Thanksgiving heralded the arrival of the holiday shopping season.

Shown here is a road grader smoothing the ground for the future Layton Commons Park on Wasatch Drive during the 1960s. Today's crown jewel of the Layton Parks System, this 47-acre oasis contains four restrooms, a one-and-a-half-mile walking trail, two playgrounds, two baseball fields, two picnic pavilions, fifteen picnic shelters, and nine barbecue grills. It is not certain how the park was named, but the title likely keys on the fact this is a park for the common people. In 1957, Layton purchased the future park land from the federal government. Many of the mature trees on the land were preserved for the new park.

This is a 1965 advertisement in the *Davis County Clipper* newspaper for Layton's Davis Drive In Theater. Located where today's Kohl's department store is, the drive-in sat on 23 acres at about 1100 North Main Street. The theater began in 1945 and closed after the 1991 season because of economic reasons. Indoor theaters and dollar theaters decreased the drive-in audience. In its heyday, some 900 cars full of viewers packed the twin screens. Neighborhoods nearby could readily hear some of the movie soundtracks on summer evenings.

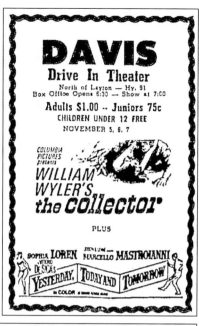

This advertisement by the Layton Chamber of Commerce appeared in the *Davis County Clipper* newspaper of May 26, 1967, heralding Layton as "a choice place to live." Layton High School, which opened a year prior, was highlighted the most. Other high notes included Layton's six elementary schools, five city parks, thirteen Latter-day Saint wards, and four other churches in town.

This is a photograph of three Layton doctors and one dentist who combined their musical skills to become a singing quartet in Davis County in the mid-20th century. They used various comical names for their group, like Three Cut-ups and a Jerk. From left to right are Dr. Robert Kelly, Dr. Robert Bitner, Dr. Robert Christensen, and Dr. De J. Cutler. All four of the men were involved with Tanner Clinic in Layton.

Shown here is an unidentified Layton policeman searching through police files in an undated Layton City photograph, probably from the 1960s. Back then, the police department was housed in some former Verdeland Park buildings, where today's Commons Park is. The mission of the Layton Police Department is to work in partnership with the community to recognize and resolve public safety concerns of all citizens by providing quality, professional service in an honest and ethical manner.

"Year Around"

LAYTON CITY'S SURF 'N SWIM

- Swimming Pool
- Racquetball Courts
- Sauna
- Steam Room

- Recreation Offices

Layton Swimming & Wave Pool Complex

437 North Wasatch Dr, Layton
(Just North of Layton High School)

Pool 546-9846
(If No Answer)
Recreation Office 544-3458

This was a Layton City advertisement from the late 1980s for its new wave pool, the Surf 'n Swim, located at 437 North Wasatch Drive. The facility opened in 1986, featuring a half-million gallons of water and surf-like wave action. The pool also had a bubble top to enclose it in comfort during the non-summer seasons and create a year-round aquatic facility. Racquetball courts, a sauna, a steam room, and recreation offices are also part of the facility.

Shown here is Layton City Council member Lyndia Graham speaking at the dedication program for the new Layton City Hall at 437 Wasatch Drive on December 28, 1990. Mayor-elect James Layton (sitting in front of the US flag) is flanked by other city officials. Layton wisely built a city hall with an unfinished basement to grow into for the coming decades.

Jerry Stevenson, Layton City councilman (left), and James Layton, mayor-elect of Layton, hold a plaque commemorating the dedication of the new Layton City Hall on December 28, 1990. That marker is on the foyer wall at city hall today.

This is a mid-1990s photograph from the I-15 bridge on Gentile Street looking east. A banner highlights the upcoming Liberty Days celebration on the Fourth of July. Klenke Floral, Burger Stop, and Pizza Hut are visible along Gentile Street.

This is a musical production in the Layton Ed Kenley Amphitheater, located in the heart of Commons Park. This performance, probably set in the late 1990s, gathered spectators from not just Layton but all over Davis County. The amphitheater opened in 1995 and was named for the late Ed Kenley of Kenley Ford, who helped fund the facility.

Weber State University cheerleaders march and exhibit their high-flying skills in the 2014 Layton Liberty Days Parade on the Fourth of July. This photograph, taken at the Fort Lane and Gentile Street intersection, shows some of the thousands of spectators who watch the parade each year. (Author photograph.)

Eight

WASATCH MOUNTAINS

The Wasatch Mountains, east of Layton City, are majestic landmarks many probably take for granted each day. However, what are the names of the mountain peaks and canyons viewed regularly? Surprisingly, the majority of the mountain peaks lack official names. Some longtime residents have opted to nickname a few of the nameless peaks. Even some of the smaller canyons are not titled.

From Weber Canyon to Farmington Canyon is the width of the main mountainous panorama that most Layton residents see daily.

The kingpin of those mountains is Thurston Peak, at 9,706 feet above sea level. However, this loftiest of peaks for both Davis and Morgan Counties was not officially named until 1993—it was previously listed as a benchmark, "Francis VABM," on all older maps. There is now a permanent monument of Utah granite located on the peak with a brass plaque, encased in concrete, that reads, "Named in honor of Thomas Jefferson Thurston, a Centerville resident who viewed the virgin valley of Morgan from the summit of the mountain in 1852 and recognized its potential for colonization. Realizing its disadvantage was its inaccessibility, in 1855, Thurston influenced others to assist him to carve a passable wagon road through Weber Canyon. He was among the first to settle in Morgan Valley and is acknowledged for bringing about its colonization."

"Layton Peak" (an unofficial name) is the first peak to the left or north of Thurston Peak and is 9,571 feet above sea level, and "Ed's Peak" (also an unofficial name) was named after Ed Ford, who lived in a hollow down below in Kaysville, east of the City Cemetery. Francis Peak, with two radar domes on top, sits at 9,515 feet, making it the fifth-highest peak in the county. The facility's base adds 55 feet, and the radar domes chip in another 60 feet for a total of 115 feet in artificial height, making the peak, some could argue, 9,630 feet above sea level. In addition, there are three small bodies of water—the Smith Creek Lakes—hidden on the east slope of the Wasatch Mountains east of Layton and Kaysville.

This is three miles up Adams Canyon, where a spectacular 30-foot waterfall on Holmes Creek roars. This is one of the most popular canyons in Davis County, and hikers jam the trailhead on weekends and holidays. The canyon is named for a pioneer, Elias Adams Sr., who had a sawmill in the area. Samuel O. Holmes, another early Layton settler, is the namesake for the creek in the canyon. (Author photograph.)

Besides the signature waterfall at the climax of an Adams Canyon hike, there's also this smaller and lesser-known water drop at the mouth of the canyon. This waterfall, probably only about 12 feet high, is almost hidden and resides below the established trail. First-time visitors have to ponder a route to the small falls by listening for the sound of rushing water below. (Author photograph.)

This is the view from the mouth of Adams Canyon looking westward into Layton City. The popularity of the trail is supported by the many cars in its dirt parking lot at the top of Oak Hills Drive. The trailhead is just east of busy Highway 89 and next to an irrigation reservoir. (Author photograph.)

This is one of the gems of Layton, the US Forest Service's Fernwood Picnic Area. Located next to the "Layton Castle," the picnic grounds also offer access to the Bonneville Shoreline Trail and other paths in the area. Fernwood opened in 1959, and the area was originally called Fernwood Flats. The elevation of Fernwood is about 5,300 feet above sea level, or almost 1,000 feet higher than the center of Layton City. (Author photograph.)

These are the radar domes atop Francis Peak, elevation 9,630 feet above sea level. They are a well-known skymark for the Layton area and North Davis County. They were constructed in the late 1950s, and this late-1970s photograph illustrates how remote and snowy these lofty outposts are. A 12-mile dirt road leads up Farmington Canyon to the radar installations. (Courtesy of Utah State Historical Society.)

To Weber Canyon

Corbett Canyon

Corbett Creek

North Fork of Kays Creek

This photograph spans the Wasatch Mountains from Weber Canyon on the north (left) to just north of Layton Peak (right and not shown). Names of the canyons and the titled mountain peaks have been labeled on this and the three other pictures that follow. Not all of the peaks

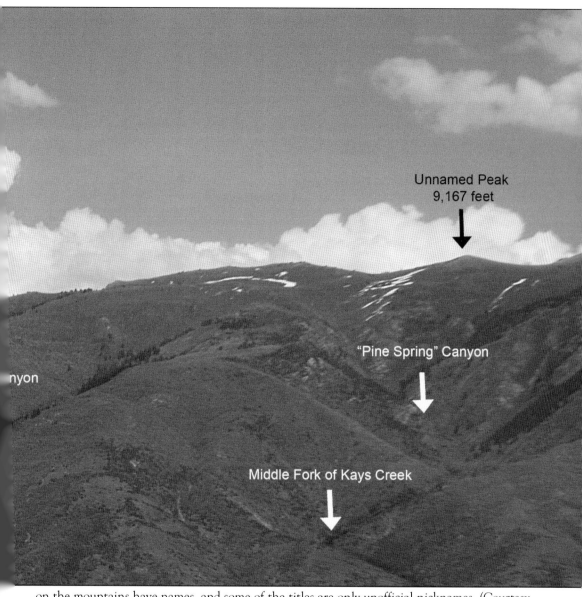

Unnamed Peak
9,167 feet

"Pine Spring" Canyon

nyon

Middle Fork of Kays Creek

on the mountains have names, and some of the titles are only unofficial nicknames. (Courtesy of Whitney Arave.)

Unnamed Peak
9,536 Feet

"Layton Peak"
9,571 Feet

"Crooked" Canyon

South Fork Kays Creek

This photograph shows the Wasatch Mountains, directly east of Layton, from an unnamed peak (left) to just past Thurston Peak, the highest point in both Davis and Morgan Counties. Besides the Bonneville Shoreline Trail spanning the foothills across these mountains, there is also the Great Western Trail, which traverses much of the mountain skyline across Davis County. There

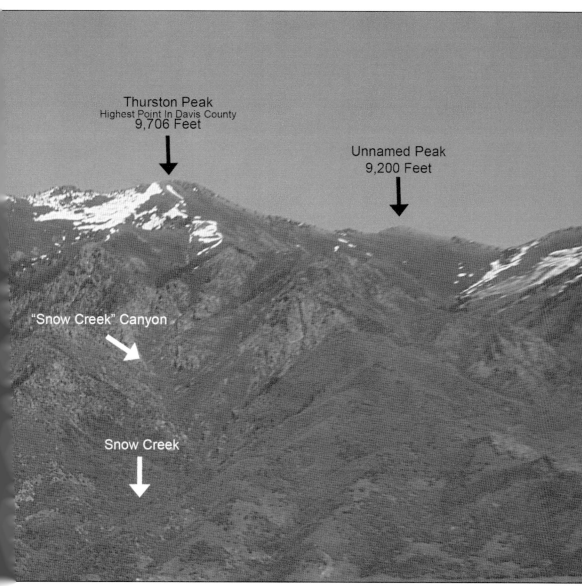

Thurston Peak
Highest Point In Davis County
9,706 Feet

Unnamed Peak
9,200 Feet

"Snow Creek" Canyon

Snow Creek

is also one obscure cabin (not shown) in this section of the Wasatch Mountains, the Fernwood Cabin, northeast of the Fernwood Picnic Area at an elevation of 6,729 feet above sea level. (Courtesy of Whitney Arave.)

Unnamed Peak
9,423 Feet

Unnamed Peak
9,491 Feet

"Snow Horse"
(Seasonal landmark)

Adams Canyon

North Fork of Holmes Creek

This section of the Wasatch Mountains east of Layton includes Adams Canyon, a popular hiking trail and the Snow Horse, located near the top of Snow Horse Ridge. There is also the obscure Adams Canyon Cabin (not shown), northeast of the Adams Canyon upper waterfall at

"Ed's" Peak
9,381

On East Side of Mountain
3 Smith Creek Lakes

Horse Ridge

Webb Canyon

Holmes Creek

an elevation of about 7,700 feet above sea level, in this section. The three Smith Creek Lakes are hidden behind the backside of the mountains, on the Morgan side. (Courtesy of Whitney Arave.)

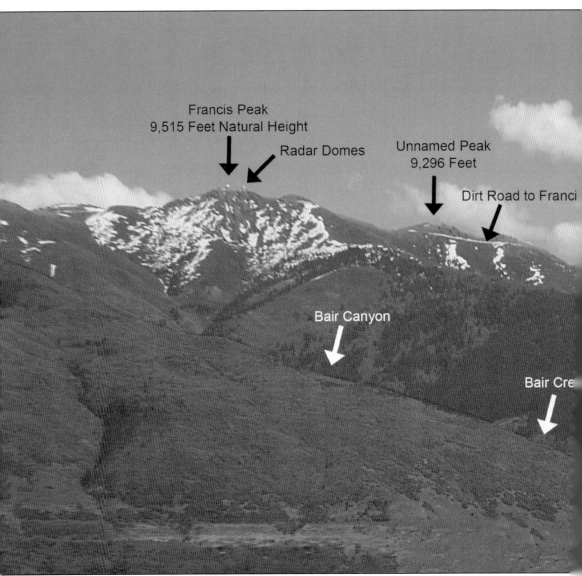

Francis Peak
9,515 Feet Natural Height

Radar Domes

Unnamed Peak
9,296 Feet

Dirt Road to Franci

Bair Canyon

Bair Cre

This photograph highlights the Francis Peak section of the Wasatch Mountains. Francis Peak was named in honor of Esther Charlotte Emily Wiesbroddt Francis, an early pioneer woman who settled in Morgan in 1863. Francis Peak was once Davis County's craggiest mountain summit. However, some 22,000 cubic yards of material and 32 feet of the peak's height were removed to

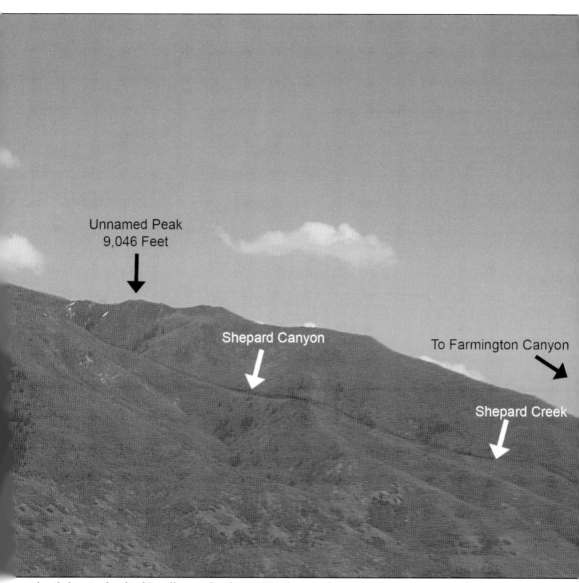

Unnamed Peak
9,046 Feet

Shepard Canyon

To Farmington Canyon

Shepard Creek

level the site for the $2-million radar domes. Workers at the peak's construction site had to wear thick, long boots and carry sticks or pistols. Although snake experts said the reptiles could not live that high, someone forgot to tell the rattlers. (Courtesy of Whitney Arave.)

This is Layton's seasonal sentinel on the mountainside, the Snow Horse, a natural shape in snow that appears almost every spring. Deep ravines on the mountain fill with snow and create the horse/colt figure. According to a story passed down by early settler Chester Flint, if any portion of the Snow Horse shape was still visible on the Fourth of July, then lower valley settlers would have stream water flowing down into autumn. More modern variations of this legend were that parents would not let their children play in the outside hose water until the Snow Horse was visible on the mountainside. Some also see a snowy bat chasing the horse underneath, while others notice a large U shape above and to the left of the Snow Horse. University of Utah sports fans especially delight in that snowy U shape. (Courtesy of Taylor Arave.)

Nine

BUSINESSES

The first two general stores in Layton's borders opened in 1882, the Farmer's Union store and the Adams and Sons Store, both on South Main Street. The First National Bank, at 12 South Main Street, Layton's former oldest continuously operating business for some 119 years (until 2019), began in 1905.

According to December 26, 1912, issue of the *Weekly Reflex* newspaper,

> Layton has business blocks that would be a credit to a much larger and more populous community, a fine new depot just completed by the Ogden Short Line Railway and a neat little depot building is nearing completion on the electric line. There are four stores handling implements and vehicles, three general stores, one drug store, a national bank, butcher shop, two restaurants, flourishing shops, pool hall, paint and wall paper house, coal yards, lumber yard and blacksmith shop.

Besides the sugar factory, which opened in 1915, Hines and Company began business in the 1920s at 1140 West Gentile Street as a produce/transportation company specializing in onions. It incorporated its business in 1936 and still operates today.

The Fort Lane Shopping Center began in 1963 at Gentile Street and Fort Lane, anchored by Safeway, Kings, and Layton Drug.

Kmart, Layton's first modern big box store, opened at Antelope and Main Streets in 1978.

The Layton Hills Mall started in 1980 and sparked a retail and restaurant boom in the area. (See Chapter 10 for more of the mall's history.)

Layton had very slim pickings for eateries back in the early 1980s. However, by the 1990s, the city was a gourmet heaven and dieter's nightmare with its famed Restaurant Row.

Within a half-mile were dozens of restaurants that offered a wide range of selections that would appeal to almost anyone.

It was not Layton's original plan to have any restaurants located north of the Layton Hills Mall. The city had hoped for a large business park in the area. There are some offices there, but the eating places just started coming in and took over the area.

Layton has become the home for numerous other businesses, but space will not permit naming them all.

This is the Ernest Layton Building, located at 27 South Main Street, which opened in 1909 and housed a hardware store on the main floor. Later, the front corner was leased to the Davis County Independent Phone Company, and the second floor was leased to three doctors for a hospital. The medical facility was only there from 1911 to 1913. Many businesses came and went there, with Dutch Maid occupying the building in the 1980s.

Shown here is the interior of the Layton Auto Company, located at 11 North Main Street, in the 1920s, complete with five employees. Lucas Laudie opened the shop in 1920, with a new 40-by-145-foot brick showroom. The Layton Post Office even rented space in the building from 1922 to 1925. The business sold Pontiac and Oakland cars. Murray Cowley purchased the auto company in 1925. The Layton City fire engine was temporarily housed in the building in 1928. George Briggs and Leonard Layton bought the business in 1931. The auto business closed in 1941, and the building was demolished in 1953 to widen Main Street.

This is Burton Implement Company in the 1920s, located at 104 North Main Street. Annie Bone is posing in front of the store. She was the daughter of Francis Bone, who worked at the store, which first opened in 1916. Charles Barber and his son Eljin Barber also helped operate the business, which did well in Layton, a farming community in that era.

Shown here is the Utah Power and Light Office and Store at 26 North Main Street, probably in the 1920s. H.J. Sheffield constructed the 30-by-60-foot brick building in 1913. The power company also sold Hotpoint appliances. Utah Power moved out in 1953 and relocated to East Gentile Street.

Robert E. Dansie and his wife, Llwellyn, began a store at 593 South Main Street in 1925, and it operated for 47 years. They initially sold groceries, ice cream, hot dogs, and gasoline. They expanded the 12-by-12-foot store several times over the years until they retired in 1972.

This is Dansie's Service Station and Store at 593 South Main Street in the 1930s. Dansie's was one of the first gas-and-go convenience-type stores in Davis County. The store also sold Brown's Ice Cream and even tires. Robert E. Dansie, who owned and operated the store with his wife, is posing in the photograph. Note how gasoline prices were not commonly posted in this era.

Here is the First National Bank of Layton (now First Community Bank Utah) at its original location of 50 West Gentile Street. This was Davis County's third bank, and this picture is likely from the 1930s. The bank was headed by E.P. Ellison with help from many local residents. It was the oldest consecutive business in Layton for more than 113 years.

This is the interior of the First National Bank of Layton at 50 West Gentile Street in the 1930s. Annie Brown, a bank teller, is on the right, while Lawrence E. Ellison is standing on the far left. The other two men are unidentified employees. The bank's original marble walls and counters were transferred to the old Farmer's Union Building at 12 South Main Street, where the bank relocated to in 1981.

Shown here is Layton's original First National Bank building, located at 50 West Gentile Street, as it appeared in the 1970s, probably just before the bank relocated across the street. Note that the building is now painted white. The bank was sold to a Montana banking company in March 2019.

This is a close-up view of Knowley Drug Store at 52 North Main Street back in 1936. The drugstore opened in 1924. Laytona Hall and Motion Picture Theater used a portion of the same building, and when moviegoers exited, it was through the drugstore, with its soda fountain and snacks. Knowley Drug closed its doors in 1980, but many weddings and socials were held in the building over the decades.

This is a partial view of the intersection of Main and Gentile Streets in Layton looking east. This photograph was probably taken in the late 1930s. The Shell service station is in the center of the picture, and the Latter-day Saint White Chapel can be seen in the distance on the left. A portion of Layton's first park, intersected by a spur line of the railroad, shows up at the bottom of the photograph.

Shown here is Staley's Lunch Café, located at 46 North Main Street in the early 1930s. It opened in 1926 and enlarged its seating in 1936. T.W. and Bessie Staley managed the café, and they branched out and opened the West Layton Cash Grocery Store in the late 1930s at 1378 West Gentile Street. However, the store only lasted a few years and closed in 1940. Next door to Staley's was Layton Drug at 40 North Main Street.

This view of Layton's Main Street looks southeast in 1936. From left to right are Knowley Drug, Henry Smedley's barbershop, Staley's Café, a pool hall, Midway Café, Dick's Service Station, and Utah Power and Light. Note how narrow Layton's Main Street was. (It wasn't widened until the 1950s.)

Here is a picture of the short-lived Travelers Café on Main Street. It began in Layton in 1952 but did not catch on or last into the 1960s. It featured lunches and dinners, ice cream, and more. This café is one of many Layton eateries that have come and gone over the decades.

This is Nalder's Sinclair Service Station, at 450 North Main Street. It was one of Layton's first modern gasoline stations. Today, Chuck E. Cheese Family Fun and Entertainment is located on the same piece of property.

DAVIS COUNTY'S FIRST AND ONLY ONE STOP SHOPPING CENTER

FARMERS UNION
OF LAYTON

Traditionally an institution of fair dealings and savings to their customers, serving them with leading quality and trade name products in . . .

—Lumber	—Appliances	—Hardware	—Dry Goods	—Groceries
—Coal	—Housewares	—Meat	—John Deere Farm Equipment	

Here is an advertisement for the Farmer's Union store at 12 South Main Street, probably in the 1940s. The store billed itself as Davis County's first and only one-stop shopping center, dating back to 1882. Selling groceries, farm equipment, lumber, coal, and everything in between, the Farmer's Union store was in business until it closed in 1957. A dentist's office, cannery store, and furniture store were later uses for the building.

This is the east side of Main Street in Layton in 1936. Prominently shown from left to right are the gun and bicycle shop; the Layton Golden Rule Store, 110 North Main Street (also subdivided into Clarence Okuda's Layton Noodle Parlor restaurant and Japanese Market, which operated from 1943 to 1961); and the Ritz Theater at 96 North Main Street, which opened in 1941 and continued until 1968, when the popularity of television closed it. (The theater building now houses Great Harvest Bread.)

Here is Mountain Fuel Supply's original work crew in its the Layton office in about 1949; from left to right are (first row) Ted Hulse, Grover Moffitt, Vern Salter, and Max Swensen; (second row) Elmo Christensen, Frank Jensen, Walter Wagner, and Rodney Lewis. The first natural gas office in Layton opened in about 1940 in part of the home at 52 East Gentile Street. An addition to the home and business was made in 1954, and in 1987, the company built a 15,000-square-foot office on Gordon Avenue, just west of Main Street. That office closed several decades later. (Note that Mountain Fuel is now renamed Dominion Energy.)

This is the interior of Max Bishop Ford, located at 110 West Gentile Street, in 1948. Note the salesman walking in the picture as well the sign promoting improved V-6 and V-8 engines. Auto sales were brisk in the late 1940s following the shortage of cars during World War II.

This was the exterior of Max Bishop Ford, located at 110 West Gentile Street. It opened on March 1, 1946. Since new cars were not manufactured during World War II, prospective buyers were put on a waiting list, and some did not receive their vehicle until 1948. Max Bishop later partnered with Ed Stromberg, and the business name then changed to B&M Ford Sales.

The Dipper was Layton's first drive-in restaurant, located on North Main Street in the 1950s and 1960s. Long before McDonald's came along, it offered hamburgers, fries, and ice cream. Del Adams owned the restaurant, and Ned Nalder was the Dipper manager for many years. The eatery also boasted a fun neon sign. The Dipper was located near the short-lived Layton Drive-In (note the large big screen of the theater rising up above the Dipper building in the picture). The Layton Drive-In, near 600 North Main Street, only operated from 1950 to 1955.

This is Wayne's Market at 300 North Gentile Street in the mid-1950s. Wayne Winegar's two sons, Bob (left) and Tom (right), dressed in full western attire, pose on a horse that the store gave away as a prize in a big promotion. The boys' dog is also standing in the lower left side of the photograph.

Here is a mid-1960s advertisement for Union Mortuaries in Davis County. The Layton Union Mortuary opened in April 1961 at 1095 North Main Street and sat on three acres of land. The mortuary's chapel, in the foreground, was added onto the south end of Ray Dawson's former home. Reid R. Holbrook was the first manager of the facility, and his family also lived in the complex, which included six viewing rooms. After the mortuary closed decades later, it was remodeled into a strip mall comprising many different small shops.

The anchor store of the original Fort Lane Shopping Center was Safeway, as shown in this 1970s photograph. Layton Drug and Kings were the two other large shops in Layton's first-ever major retail development at Fort Lane and Gentile Streets. Safeway was eventually replaced by several other stores, including Food for Less. Today, Winco Foods and other shops and restaurants are located on the same property.

This was the artist's conception of the original design for the Layton Hills Mall in the late 1970s. The plans did not quite match the drawing, but when the mall opened in 1980, it sparked retail growth in the area by becoming the catalyst for other stores and restaurants locating on the mall's ring road and also for the future Restaurant Row, to the north. Although many businesses have changed in the area over the decades, the mall remains a thriving enterprise in an era when many other malls in the United States have closed.

Kim Sill, one of the owners of Layton's Sill's Café, stands in the back of a pickup truck at the front of the café at 281 South Main Street, probably in the 1980s. The café, Layton's oldest eatery (overlooking some lapses in operation), started in 1957. Sill's soon became the local favorite, especially among farmers. Its huge, delicious scones are legendary. In 2009, Sill's had to relocate when the Utah Department of Transportation constructed the Layton Parkway. The café reopened later in a former Pizza Hut building at 335 East Gentile Street.

This is Layton's expanded Main Street, with four lanes in a divided highway configuration, as pictured in 1961. *The Sword of Sherwood Forest* was playing at the Layton Theater at the time the picture was taken. The picture looks south towards the intersection with Gentile Street.

The Smith's Food (Kroger) Plant and Distribution Center at 500 North Sugar Street opened in 1985. The ice cream plant was added in 1990. Semitrucks are commonly spotted on Sugar Street and West Hill Field Road going to and from the Smith's Warehouse. (Author photograph.)

Tanner Clinic is likely the oldest continuous business in Layton City. It began at 418 West Gentile Street with Dr. A.Z. Tanner. He built a brick home with an office and waiting room there. Following his death, his son Dr. Noall Z. Tanner used the office until he constructed a new facility named Tanner Memorial Clinic at 317 West Gentile Street in 1947. The current flagship Tanner Clinic building opened at 2120 North 1700 West in 1977. The clinic has six other satellite locations and plans for more. (Author photograph.)

Wimmer's Sewing & Vacuums is probably Layton's second-oldest continuous business, having started in 1922. Ace Wimmer founded the business in Layton, and now it is in its fourth generation of family members. Spencer Carter, a great-grandson-in-law, now owns the business, located at 1078 East Gentile Street. Wimmer also has a second store in Ogden. (Author photograph.)

Ten

MODERN CITY

Modern Layton City is a community that has truly been built on two "Hills"—Hill Air Force Base and the Layton Hills Mall—to become Davis County's largest town as well as a regional shopping hub.

First, there was Hill Field. The US Congress approved $8 million in July 1939 to establish the Ogden Air Depot. Six months later, in December, the War Department selected the name Hill Field in honor of the late Maj. Ployer Hill, who had perished in an experimental aircraft accident in 1935.

An official ground breaking was held on January 12, 1940, and the facility was built and expanded from there. Layton's first subdivisions, Hill Villa, Skyline, and Ellison, came along in 1941. Layton also experienced a business boom in 1946, following World War II, with its expanded population. By 1947, the Army Air Corps became the US Air Force, and Hill Field was renamed Hill Air Force Base.

The Layton Hills Mall is Layton's other significant "hill." "Work set to begin on Layton Hills Mall" was an August 4, 1978, headline in the *Davis County Clipper*. The mall was then described as a mammoth indoor shopping center with some surrounding businesses, conveniently next to Interstate 15. It opened after more than two years of construction. Some of the land eventually developed into the Layton Hills Mall used to be the old 20-acre Layton Trailer Park. The Layton Hills Mall opened in the spring of 1980 and was renovated in 1996. Though it is not on an actual hill, the mall has, over the decades, help attract many more businesses to Layton.

Layton's size in square miles grew from 1.75 at incorporation in 1920 to 5.8 in 1938, to 10.0 in 1970, to 12.0 in 1981, to 17.4 in 1985, and finally to 22.49 in 2019.

Layton has annexed two other communities over the decades: Laytona in 1957 and East Layton in 1984. Layton City erected a new city municipal building and complex in Commons Park, and it was dedicated in 1990.

This aerial view of Layton with east at top was taken in the early 1990s and spotlights Layton High School, Commons Park, and Layton City Hall in the center of the picture. Layton High's circular track distinctly shows up, as does Interstate 15 and numerous subdivisions in the area.

This is a section of eastern Layton City as it appeared in an aerial view of the 1990s looking west. Oak Hills Drive is the straight road on the left of the picture. It also shows Company Pond (bottom), East Gentile Street winding around the water, the Valley View Golf Course, and the many homes in the area. Adams Reservoir is at the top of the picture. Company Pond, also known as Holmes Reservoir, was begun as a dam in 1852 and is one of the nation's oldest reservoirs.

Layton City is home to the Davis Conference Center, located at 1651 North 700 West. The $11-million center opened in 2004 and caters to conventions, conferences, meetings, weddings, large funerals, dining events, and more. The Davis Conference Center is a 110,000-square-foot convention/conference center with over 70,000 square feet of flexible meeting space. It is located in the heart of Layton's hotel district as well as conveniently near Restaurant Row, with a wide variety of eateries. (Author photograph.)

This is a lofty view of Layton's downtown historic district in 2014. Taken from the upper floor of some apartments under construction, the picture looks northeast. Some of the historic buildings from the early 1900s are still in use on Main Street. Also note the many trees in town. (Author photograph.)

This is the Layton Midtown Crossing bridge over Interstate 15, which opened in style on June 25, 2018. Layton City, Davis County, and state officials hold the banner before a procession of vehicles crosses the overpass. The $25-million project at 1300 North and 1425 West features a 293-foot-long bridge over the freeway and offers new access from Main Street to Hill Field Road and in between. (Author photograph.)

This is the logo designed to commemorate Layton City's 100th birthday as an official city. Layton separated from Kaysville in 1902, but it was not until May 24, 1920, that Layton City officially incorporated as its own town. Layton planned celebrations in the spring of 2020 to note its century mark.

This is the front of Layton City's offices, at 437 North Wasatch Drive. Rising upwards at the front of the building is *Two Boys on Stilts*, a unique statue the city acquired in the early 1990s. This bronze sculpture is often unnoticed and unheralded, blending in so well with the surroundings. This sculpture—now symbolizing an upward-looking city, including many children—was created by Lindon, Utah, artist Dennis Smith in 1980. It was intended for a business that relocated out of state, and so the sculpture ended up in front of city hall in the early 1990s.

Shown here are pockets of farmland that still exist in Layton City today amidst sprawling subdivisions. This area shown in west Layton highlights the mixture of rural v. urban development. Most of Layton's farmers today live on the west side of town, but they are gradually on the decrease. (Author photograph.)

Hill Air Force Base is seen here in 2015 from the Wasatch Mountain foothills in east Layton. Hill AFB is located on a hill (elevation 4,800 feet above sea level) that was formerly part of what pioneer ranchers called "the Sandridge." Hill AFB is Utah's largest single-site employer, and its economic impact on the state is over $3 billion annually. (Author photograph.)

This is the Heritage Museum of Layton in Commons Park. The museum includes rotating displays and antique items. Some of the many relics on display include a 1903 Runabout car, an old phonograph, a piano, a stove, and even vintage Barbie dolls. (Author photograph.)

About the Heritage Museum of Layton

Many of the photographs in this book are courtesy of the Heritage Museum of Layton. Back in 1972, a group of concerned citizens decided to build a Layton museum. They formed a museum nonprofit 501(c)(3) corporation to raise money for a museum building, selected an ideal museum location, gathered artifacts, constructed a museum building with private donations, and then once the museum building was completed and paid for, donated the building and the artifact collection to Layton City as a permanent home for the cultural heritage items of Layton's history.

The museum opened to the general public in August 1980 at 403 North Wasatch Drive in Commons Park, across from Layton High School.

Over time, the museum's heritage collection has grown to include 2,470 artifact objects, 3,770 historical photographs, 2,900 archival documents, and 299 books.

Admission to the museum is free. Its hours are 11:00 a.m. to 6:00 p.m. Tuesday through Friday and 11:00 a.m. to 5:00 p.m. on Saturdays. It is closed Sunday, Monday, and holidays. Visit the museum's website at laytoncity.org/LC/HeritageMuseum.

Discover Thousands of Local History Books
Featuring Millions of Vintage Images

Arcadia Publishing, the leading local history publisher in the United States, is committed to making history accessible and meaningful through publishing books that celebrate and preserve the heritage of America's people and places.

Find more books like this at
www.arcadiapublishing.com

Search for your hometown history, your old stomping grounds, and even your favorite sports team.